imagined
landscapes

Josef Pachner b. 23.1.87 d. 8.9.42   Anna Pachnerová b. 8.6.89 d. 8.9.42   Karel Pachner b. 17.5.20 d. 8.9.42

FLORIDA HOLOCAUST MUSEUM
55 Fifth Street South, St. Petersburg, Florida 33701

ISBN 0-9700333-2-X

Designer: Ann Pachner 212.673.5686
Printed in China through Colorcraft Ltd., Hong Kong
Photography: All photos Karen Mibus; except Maja Kihlstedt p.13, 18, 19, 21, 22, 23, 24, 37, 43, 59; Jennifer Elliot p.5.

Our mission statement:

The Florida Holocaust Museum honors the memory of millions of innocent men, women, and children who suffered or died in the Holocaust. The Museum is dedicated to teaching the members of all races and cultures the inherent worth and dignity of human life in order to prevent future genocides.

The Door

reface

Retrospective exhibitions are meant to present seminal junctures in an artist's career. These are the defining points that, in the best of all worlds, establish the artist's career, his or her work and the place of that work in the larger galaxy of art.

William Pachner has reached yet another juncture that is significant – in the not-too-distant future he will celebrate his 90th birthday. This is significant by itself but is made ever so much more so because of his history and the under-lying story told by his paintings, drawings and collages. William Pachner came to this country from his native Czechoslovakia in 1939 full of the brash enthusiasm of a young artist/illustrator set on a career in advertising and magazine illustration in America. Whatever thoughts he may have had of returning home were never to be realized. Adolph Hitler and his war machine destroyed any possible hope of going home again when they invaded Czechoslovakia. Pachner was never to see any of his family again. Not one family member survived the Holocaust.

William Pachner made a life out of tragedy – but he never forgot his family or the world of his youth. After a suc-cessful early career in magazine illustration, which included searing anti-war and anti-Nazi cartoons and carica-tures, Bill aggressively sought to join the art world of New York. Here, too, he succeeded with group and solo exhi-bitions in New York. Eventually, his work made it into America's leading museums. His career blossomed as did his personal life. He married Lorraine and they had two children. After 1952, his mountainside in Woodstock remained home; but the winter months were spent on Florida's Gulf Coast. His familial past stayed with him, and his paintings continued to resonate with these subliminal echoes.

Look at Bill Pachner's paintings closely and you will see trees morphing into figures, sometimes tortured and writhing, while others stand firm and resolute. There are scarred and worn landscapes that were once verdant and luscious. And then, there are his trucks and trains—most in black and white—painted when his eyesight began to fail him in the early 1980s. Trucks and trains, which were really the only means of transportation throughout 20th Century Europe, became the vehicles of conveyance to death in the concentration and death camps of Nazi Germany. Somehow, though, Bill Pachner made them strong, powerful and beautiful in his own superlative way. Perhaps in his language, they are a tribute to his family, and so many others, lost to the Holocaust.

In the end, who is Bill Pachner? He is first and foremost an artist and, as all artists, he has a story to tell. He also is a "survivor"—the sole representative of a lost family. So, are the works pastoral landscapes of Woodstock, NY or are they requiems for the past? Regardless of how one views his work, Bill Pachner is a master artist, an intellectual with taste, eloquence and consummate style. We first met almost twenty years ago and he hasn't changed one iota. He doesn't even look older!

So, this *is* a seminal moment. Bill Pachner wishes us to remember his work, his life, and his compelling **_Imagined Landscapes_**.

R. Andrew Maass, Executive Director

WILLIAM PACHNER:

Imagined Landscapes

"Absence is the highest form of presence."—James Joyce

"The past is never dead, it is not even past."—William Faulkner, *Requiem for a Nun*

"Try again. Fail again. Fail better."—Samuel Beckett, *Worstward Ho*

At the beginning of the twentieth century, there was considerable optimism around the world because of a belief that technology and scientific innovation could improve the lives of humanity. Unfortunately, the same technology that was supposed to provide a road to utopia also provided a pathway for the destructive forces of war, racism, hatred and mass murder.

If any group saw the potential for disaster, it was the artists. Even before the guns of August 1914, painters such as Ludwig Meidner had apocalyptic visions in their paintings. The great German Expressionists Otto Dix, George Grosz, Hannah Hoch, Kathe Kollwitz, Ernst Ludwig Kirchner and Max Beckmann also saw a deeper and darker vision of humanity emerge from the trenches of World War I, as if a prediction of more dire things to come. For a few, however, being part of the atrocities at the front was an elevating experience. In the German case, the war became the basis of national resurrection and helps explain the absence of a monument to an unknown soldier in Germany after 1918 as well the pursuit of genocide as a "glorious enterprise" linked to a group of men who saw mass murder as an aesthetic exercise.

American artist William Pachner, now approaching his ninth decade, was born into this environment on April 7, 1915. The Austro-Hungarian Empire into which he was born evaporated in 1918. However, there was optimism at hand in the newly formed Czechoslovak democracy under Thomas Masaryk. Brtnice, his Moravian birthplace, provided the young Pachner with a loving family environment, a sense of history and a landscape that has never left his memory. He has said that the Czech highlands provided him with a sense of spiritual connectedness to the soil that was mirrored when he moved to Woodstock, New York in 1945.

The "Jewish question" and Jewish identity did not weigh heavily on the young Pachner until Hitler came to power in neighboring Germany. Pachner's Jewish roots were modern, meaning less dependent on religion and stronger in individual identity. Jews in the Czech lands were emancipated in 1867 and by the late 1920s and

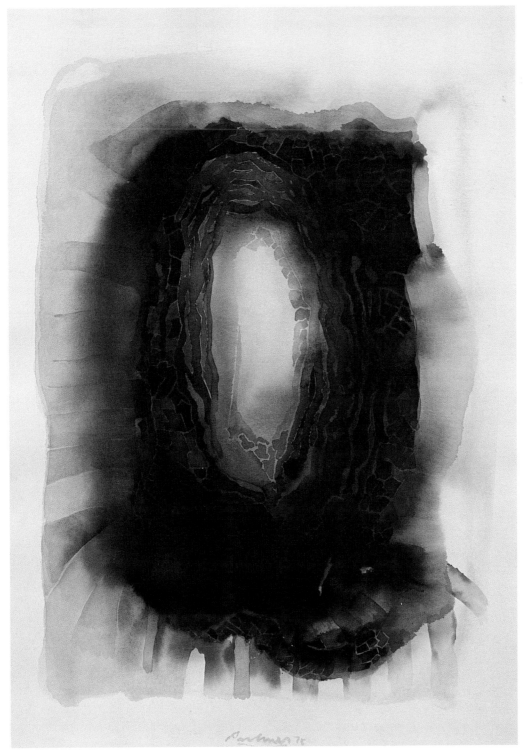

Elegy for a City

His Spiritual Highness

early 1930s, Czechoslovakia, even outside of Prague, created an environment that spawned intellectual creativity. Gustav Mahler was born in Kalist, Bohemia, and his family moved to Jihlava, next door to Pachner's hometown. Sigmund Freud was born in Freiberg, Moravia, while Franz Kafka was born and lived his whole life in Prague. Enigmatic Jewish identities were solidified by outsiders who made their own determinations of who were Jews and who were not.

Trained as an illustrator, Pachner moved to Prague and eventually left Czechoslovakia for the United States in 1939. When World War II broke out, he realized he could not return, and a large and everlasting absence became part of his being. The artist himself has said, "…the connectedness was of lasting and determining importance—a bond of intimate and life-giving connection, which intensified with its loss."

During World War II, Pachner prospered by becoming art director for *Esquire,* later doing illustrations for *Collier's, Cosmopolitan* and other national magazines. His attempts to join the armed forces failed because of limited vision in one eye. The magazine illustrations from this period, however, are instructive as they were drawn often to accompany texts about the war and Nazi atrocities. Without having seen the events of what we now call the Holocaust, Pachner's drawings and illustrations captured the horror with remarkable accuracy and had an indelible impact. Pachner illustrated an article by Jan Karski entitled "Polish Death Camp," in the October 14, 1944 edition of *Collier's* Magazine. Karski had come to the United States on a mission from the Polish underground. While here, he also spoke with President Roosevelt about the extermination of the Jews. His accounts were those of an eyewitness, as he had been smuggled into the death camp at Belzec dressed in an Estonian uniform. Pachner's frightful illustration shows a torrent of Jews being loaded from a platform into already overstuffed German Railroad boxcars for deportation to their death. Manuel Komroff, writing in 1944 about Pachner's illustrations for these stories of Nazi atrocities, commented: "Let us not forget. And let us not forgive. Pachner's pictures are not easy to forget…. Now that millions know, they will not forget. And they cannot possibly forgive." Pachner's illustration of a deportation, an "imagined landscape" of sorts, was as accurate as any photograph taken of this crime by the perpetrators themselves.

Inquisitor

After the war, Pachner abandoned a lucrative career doing illustration to become a studio artist. He divided his time between Woodstock, New York and Florida's Gulf Coast. Pachner discovered Woodstock by accident when on a train ride from New York to Chicago on the famed New York Central Railroad's "Twentieth Century Limited." The landscape reminded him of his home. Only later did he discover that it was an art colony. While he knew many artists, he never considered himself an insider because of its politics and artistic rivalries. He did, however associate with likeminded individuals. These

German Train

A Word from Our Sponsor

included Eugene Speicher, who was sometimes called "the dean of the Woodstock painters," and had been a fellow student with Edward Hopper, Rockwell Kent, Guy Pen du Bois, George Bellows and Georgia O'Keeffe. The dialogue which emerged from his friendship with Italian sculptor Alfeo Faggi, and his next-door neighbor painter Yasuo Kuniyoshi (a victim of much discrimination by Americans during the war years), and Philip Guston, proved to be of lasting importance, as was the moral support and steadfast encouragement of the artist, Edward L. Chase.

What affected Pachner most was going to museums, self-education and a long arduous process of reading, study, and contemplating a landscape that recalled his home and family. Pachner's painting of the post-war period contained many different approaches: satiric drawings; as well as a large body of an erotic, celebratory nature; figurative paintings; Biblical Judaic and Christian themes; photo-montages; and paintings of great color intensity. The seductive color juxtaposition had instant and broad appeal to those who viewed paintings in purely decorative terms. Seeking a balance, he embraced the full range of human experience in the world—the light as well as the dark, the joyous and the tragic.

In this immediate post-war period, Pachner also produced many satiric photomontages that critiqued bourgeois sensibilities, taste, and consumerism. These works made indictments of individuals and organizations for their complicity in recent atrocities. For example, *His Spiritual Highness in a State of Moral Dilemma* (1949) is his comment on the failure of Pope Pius XII and the Vatican to condemn Nazism and call Christian conscience to bear on the mass murder of the Jews. The discourse that surrounds the role of the Vatican and Nazism is still contentious. *Inquisitor* is a similar work that reminds us there is a long history of authoritarian suppression of dissident views. Pachner's mixed-media work, especially the photomontages of this period, were most analogous to the pre-war satirical artist John Heartfield, whose works, published in European magazines, understood the evil of Nazism and its criminal intent from the outset. Two of Pachner's satirical works, *A Group of Winning Sportsmen* (1953) and *A Word from Our Sponsor* (1962), are biting critiques of the post-war materialism and high self-regard of the new corporate elites and their families. *Chamber of Commerce Meeting in Miami* (1961) is a cartoon-like look at an overstuffed America's capitalist elite who presume to be the arbiters of artistic taste. *The Collector*, a 1961 photomontage, pokes fun at the art collector who purchases any work by famous artists, such as Mondrian, Chagall, Miro and Pollack, to raise his own presumed status in the community. The unidentified collector sits in the middle, shirt open, eating a TV dinner (popular in the 1950s), while a large plate of spaghetti and meatballs appears to be the foundation block of the entire art collection.

Pachner's work during this period also reflect his serious side. *Family by the Graveside* (1955) is a colorful watercolor, but also a painting that depicts a family, men and women of every age, dressed in every style of clothing, including a woman with her breasts nearly exposed, under a tent at graveside. A rabbi, identified by skullcap, reads from a text. However, the body of the deceased is out of view and one might speculate the grave is

A group of winning sportsmen.

Family at Grave Site

empty, suggesting that memory of the life of the deceased is short among the living. This painting is in the tradition of the painters of earlier periods, what has been called *momento mori,* a reminder that no matter how serene and optimistic we find our present circumstances, one cannot forget that in the midst of life we are reminded of the inevitability of death. Pachner's figures in this watercolor appear desensitized by the funeral as if it is a fate they can escape.

Pachner's inner conflicts about himself as both immigrant and artist can be found in two small works: *Double Portrait of the Artist* (1945) and *Emigrant Portrait of the Artist* (1961). The former, with two figures, is drawn in the style of *Esquire* cartoon figures of the era, with accents of brown and gray color. The figure on the left, working happily on his canvas, while a scantily clad woman dances to his left. The second figure is inverted, has an angry face, wears cowboy boots with spurs, holds a knife in an attack position while striking at what appears to be an abstract form and a group of four workers dressed in blue carrying a wordless placard. An image of the scales of justice hangs from the artist's palette while an inverted scales of justice seems to be attached to his left knee and appears as a parachute. The work suggests Pachner's desire to remain focused on aesthetics and to disassociate himself from the anger and religious-like debates about socialism that were part of the intellectual debate within the artistic community. After the war, many intellectuals continued to espouse the cause of Socialism and often followed a Stalinist position. Pachner always insisted that Marxism had many interpretations, not simply one decreed from Stalin. For not conforming to any party line, he became an outsider. *Emigrant Portrait of the Artist* (1961) has a torn black and white photographic image of a destroyed interior space with fireplace, debris strewn on the floor and a debarked tree branch holding up part of the ceiling

The Collector

on the left side. On the right is a loosely drawn self-portrait of the artist working at an easel. The word "EMIGRANT," cut from a newspaper, is glued at the bottom, upside down. The word "Counteroffensive," also cut from a newspaper, is glued to the image vertically at bottom right. As Pachner's own fragmented autobiography seems to appear in these works, one must ask how he continued to paint with such burdens of memory.

Many of Pachner's paintings are landscapes, sometimes approached from the ground, other times from a bird's eye view. For Pachner, landscape, especially its twentieth century alteration by mankind, reveals essential historical truths. In a certain sense, the idea of landscape, whether seen from the ground or the air, provides some re-enactment of history, albeit in a fragmented and often disjointed, nonlinear narrative. For those who have lived and been affected directly in the century of genocide, the trauma is ongoing. The landscape, although it may now be beautiful, is forever marred by memories of absence and horror. Though the blood shed on the earth of Europe does not reveal itself, the perception and memory of the artist can lead us to under-

18

stand disruptions and offenses. Pachner's landscapes from the 1950s through the 1970s often had innocuous titles, but one can speculate they contained meanings within the visual text. *The Train* (1960) is a beautiful black patchwork view of a passing train. The title is ambiguous. But even without the title, the image conveys a sense of disturbance. *Summer Landscape* (1960-67), by contrast, is bright and seemingly optimistic, with patches of white, dark greens, black and occasional small bursts of burnt orange. The painting, however, poses some questions. For example, what are the sources of the bursts of white found on a summer landscape? The repetitive aspects of these images, such as in *Landscape of Crisis* (1964), also suggests that if we look quickly at a familiar scene, it would be easy to miss the changes that man can make or has made.

Spring Landscape (1964) approaches total abstraction with a white center surrounded by brown and black fields, while *Landscape of the River Sola* (1966), an aerial scene of patchwork countryside, can be viewed simply as a multi-colored landscape depicting farmlands, roads and a river. A greater understanding of why the artist painted this particular site, largely from his imagination, can be found in an absent footnote about the Sola River. The Sola River flows next to the Auschwitz death camp. How are we to juxtapose the artist's search for a pure aesthetic in a landscape when the choice of title has the capacity to convey that which is hidden? Even Pachner's works with high color suggest such a disturbance. *Landscape* (1981), a highly colorful forest scene seems to focus upon a burning red fire at its center. Later works, especially those in black and white from the 1980s and 1990s, have simple yet complex titles like *Smashed Window* (1997) or *Door Open and Slammed Shut* (1993). The view from the interior is ambiguous and conflicted. In contrast, *Howling Forest* (1987) suggests more strongly what the landscape has witnessed; the forest becomes imbued with the events that took place there. Other versions of this theme suggest trees with human characteristics that seem to scream. *Landscape, Entirely Man Made* (1991) shows a natural landscape altered by railroad ties, curved rails and a watchtower.

Pachner's sense of landscape and memory cannot be ignored. It informs his late obsession with the powerful black and white painted or collaged works about trains, trucks, views from windows and doorways. Pachner experiences what Simon Schama calls "moments of recognition," when the traumatic past returns with a vengeance. Schama explains this as a moment "when a place suddenly exposes its connections to an ancient and peculiar vision of the forest, the mountain, or the river. A curious excavator of traditions stumbles over something protruding above the surface of the commonplaces of contemporary life. He scratches away, discovering bits and pieces of a cultural design that seems to elude coherent reconstitution but which leads him deeper into the past." Schama also notes that landscapes especially speak to a special and powerful yearning: "The craving to find in nature a consolation for our mortality."

Pachner's loss of sight beginning in 1981 has perhaps dictated the cruelest fate for the artist. He continued working in black and white until 1999, when the remainder of his vision vanished. The loss of vision was yet one more displacement. Pachner was already keenly aware that he had been displaced among cultures.

Pachner's cessation of painting in 1999 ended a cycle that began in what he refers to as his "pre-literate state of existence." As a child, he begged his grandfather to take him to the local railroad yards. The sight of this powerful means of transportation, found in the art of many artists of the 1920s and 1930s, had an immense influence on him. Early on, he began drawing tracks, and magnificent steam locomotives that billowed black smoke. There is irony here because in his youth, Pachner understood that railroads were to bring people together or to travel to inaccessible places, thereby exposing all to other cultures. The artist has remarked in a nostalgic way, "What a great and wonderful thing it was!"

Now from the perspective of the twenty-first century, Pachner understands and has tried to convey, in his latest works, not only the power and magnetism that railroads exerted on him, but also a recognition of the great illusion associated with the humane conveyance of people. These same railroads became arteries of death, having brought millions of people to killing sites and concentration camps. The viewer can easily see this unconcealed recognition in the black and white images. *Scream* (1989), *Mercedes* (1988), *Truck* (1989), *Steam Engine* (early 1990s), *Night Freight* (1993) and *Locomotive-Freight Train* (1992) are included in this exhibition and catalogue. None of these are literal renditions of a technology. His trucks and locomotives seem to scream at us. Others, with their intense speed, appear to self-destruct while engaged in their hateful passages to death and destruction.

Everyone in Pachner's family was destroyed after being deported from Prague to a little-known Belarus killing site at Maly Trostinec. Between 206,000 to 546,000 people were killed here in gas vans and by shooting, including 69,677 Jews from Bohemia and Moravia. What happened during this period confirms that almost every technology can be turned into signifiers of an absence—an absence that is intensely painful because it contains the memory of what used to be there, but is no longer. Most significantly, the artist is providing a warning for all who gaze on these images. In *The Door* (1984), a cloaked and overtly clear image communicates this warning. The black and white work in tempera shows a locked and partially disintegrated, European-stylized house door. The compositional elements of this work play some tricks on the viewer, as the door can easily be misconstrued as another aerial landscape. However, the door is "graffitied" with the words "zid!,"—the Slavic derogatory term for Jews, and the word "Jew," as well as indications of a partial star at the top.

Pachner's last works, collectively called *Exitus Aetatis Vaporis: The End of the Age of Steam,* are arguably the strongest paintings of his career. He might have chosen a title such as *Catastrophe,* the name of Samuel Beckett's last play, which is only four pages long and is considered a minimalist approach to theater. Pachner's removal of color other than black and white mirror Beckett's minimalism. Another analogy is to the landmark documentary film by French film-

Track (1966)

Native Landscape

The Train

Spring Landscape

maker Claude Lanzmann, *SHOAH*, which Pachner has never seen. Lanzmann and Pachner have something in common. For both, those trains are still moving. Manmade landmarks that we often take for granted—tracks, stations, switches, terminals, insignias such as DRB ("Deutsche Reichsbahn Gesellschaft/German State Railways")—can no longer be considered neutral objects. They reflect a historical truth about a horrific period that many would like to ignore or forget.

There are no myths here, but there is an element of mystical re-enactment in Pachner's uncomfortable commentary of history and society. The artist's sense of working and reworking through similar themes suggests an obsession with the subject and its meaning to the viewers. Pachner has noted that "everything is represented in these last paintings—the loss of eyesight, family, homeland—everything." But the loss of eyesight is something he has embraced as a form of destiny, a script that is penned down. Pachner has also said: "I have never felt the urge to give expression to any rage as Dylan Thomas wrote about his blind father: 'Do not go gently into the dark night, rage rage at the dying of the light.' I never felt that. I did not resist nor deny anything. I accept, moreover, I embrace equally the desired as well as the unbidden." Pachner also believes that the works will survive him well because his essence is in them.

However, Pachner's last paintings may be more than uncomfortable. There are elements of speed in these works. There is a speed mixed with violence, bitterness and evil. *Train and Tunnel* (1992) shows the type of box cars used in Nazi deportations, with windows covered with bars, streaking into a dark tunnel. The blackness of the tunnel suggests no exit. Working on these furious engines may even have been a process of liberation or affirmation for Pachner, for the essential theme evolved with the onset of declining vision. More than fifteen years ago Pachner noted that:

> "Following the revelations of what the Germans accomplished during the war years, I felt such a profound need to reaffirm, to say: You did not exterminate us. You crushed all our blossoms, but our roots where we derive our strength are there, beneath the scorched earth. You slaughtered them, but their terrible and profound hope lives on."

Pachner's words voice the powerlessness of the artist and the world during the Holocaust, but also the power of not forgetting. Some earlier critics have interpreted Pachner's last images of powerful locomotives as self-portraits, just as Picasso used the bull as a symbolic self-portrait. This may be the case. But there is more. When looked at as a whole, William Pachner's work is a silent elegy or perhaps a lamentation that implies challenges for the artistic community today. Pachner's works suggest that the power of the artist lies in refusing to forget those crushed aspirations, those slaughtered millions. His career, from early social commentary to late expressionism, is symbolic of the challenges that have faced every artist in our time: the balancing of a critical response to the human condition with the formal demands of art.

Stephen C. Feinstein
Guest Curator, Florida Holocaust Museum
Director, Center for Holocaust and Genocide Studies
University of Minnesota

ALL THAT IS LOST

Michael Perkins

*L*ike a locomotive disappearing down the tracks of the hours and days just passed, and then the tracks rusting, the wooden ties rotting, everything vanishes. Eventually, everything is forgotten: the rise and fall of empires, the systematic destruction of whole peoples, the faces of the beloved and the damned. All that holds the past in our minds during our brief passage is memory and art.

As his close friend for over thirty years, I can attest to William Pachner's remarkable memory. Even at his advanced age Bill can pluck from the river of time a day in 1932, aboard a train for Vienna, and describe in perfect detail the landscape he looked out on, what he smelled and heard and thought about it. He can recall every name he's encountered, every book he's read, every painting he's loved. Above all, he remembers the history of the murderous century we have recently escaped. It haunts his late black and white work.

Implicit in all works of art is the artist's decision that *this* is to be saved—this precious moment quickly vanishing; and great art stops time, stretches and fixes that chosen moment. The title of Proust's masterpiece, *In Search Of Lost Time*, puts succinctly the mission of artists like Pachner. While his career has encompassed many subjects and styles, from illustrations and satiric to erotic landscapes and large abstract black and white works, any summary of his career will come up short if it does not recognizes that Pachner's major effort has been this search for all that is lost.

Transience is his theme, and it is this great theme that enabled him to make what must, I believe, be called great art.

But, I am a poet, not an art critic, so let me write a few notes about my friend from a literary and personal point of view. Bill is extremely erudite, and carefully spoken. His playful approach to American English is Nabokovian in its sweep. Highbrow or lowbrow, he rings all the linguistic keys, dazzling his innocent interlocutors with accents, jokes, and references that sail over the heads of most. (He has no patience for fools, but far from being snobbish, he treasures workmen and seeks the company of honest, ordinary folk.)

When I met Bill in summer, 1973, I was drawn to him by his use of the language. Our instant rapport was based on a shared love of literature. Despite a lifelong passionate interest in art, I did not pretend to know much about modern painting. Bill often twitted me for my inability to see as he did—and he had only one eye. I was 31 then, Bill 58; improbably, a young poet from Appalachia and a Vienna art school-trained painter from Moravia began a dialogue and a friendship that has endured.

Through countless summer afternoons sitting on the lawn of his Woodstock home, Bill and I have shared our love of good conversation—apparently a dead art in the Age of Media—and life's reminders of transience: the loss of his eyesight and then his beloved wife, Lorraine. We spoke of our reading—Robert Musil, Samuel Beckett, Karl Kraus among so many—of local Woodstock history, world history, art; we tried to avoid politics and gossip, but sometimes we indulged. We had a good time at each meeting, perhaps because we almost always agreed: the human race is hopeless, but we must celebrate our humanity against the always-gathering forces of darkness; and an artist must do his job of reminding those who can still feel of the extraordinary preciousness of each passing moment.

And, of course, we spoke of the Holocaust. History had swept his family away, and the world of his youth, but he has never succumbed to bitterness. His revenge for these horrors has been to paint well and to live well—and to speak his mind.

To survive, above all.

Hanging in his Woodstock living room is Bill's last painting—actually collage and drawing, but executed as a painting— and seeing it, truly seeing it, is a frightening experience. As his eye sight faded, dire necessity intensified his vision into one final statement.

Although he always enjoyed being outdoors in the paradise of moss, meadow, rushing brook and woodpiles he has created over a lifetime in homage to his natal environment, since his blindness his art has become nurturing the landscape around his house, where he knows every stem of grass, every pebble. When we sit talking on his lawn he pulls up grass obsessively. Blind he sees what is needed in each corner of this landscape painting, and touches it up as with a paint brush.

As he approaches ninety, Bill is above all an artist. He works from dawn to dusk *painting* his living landscape. He *reads* (via tape recordings) great literature; his intellect is clear and often fierce. He remains youthfully irreverent. He is the smartest man I know—not because of his erudition or wit, although these are formidable, as I've noted—but because he has raged against forgetfulness and the dying of the light: because he has stayed alive to bear witness to all that is lost. Because he has prevailed, and his art is here for all to see.

—**Michael Perkins** is a poet, novelist and critic. He has published five collections of poetry, including *I Could Walk All Day* (2002). Among his many works of fiction are *Burn* (2002) and *Evil Companions* (2003). *The Secret Record*, literary criticism, was published by William Morrow in 1976. His selected criticism, *The Good Parts*, appeared in 1994. His poems and essays have appeared in *The Village Voice, The Nation, Mother Jones, Paper, Notre Dame Review, Paradoxa, American Book Review, Talisman,* and in many online magazines. June 15 2004.

Door Opened and Slammed Shut

Landscape of the River Sola

Summer Landscape

Landscape (1981)

Italian Landscape

Imagined Landscape

Lannscape of Crisis

Following images are:

Landscape, Entirely Man Made
Howling Forest
The Scream
Mercedes
Truck II
Locomotive-Freight Train
Steam Engine (early 1990's)
Train and Tunnel
Night Freight

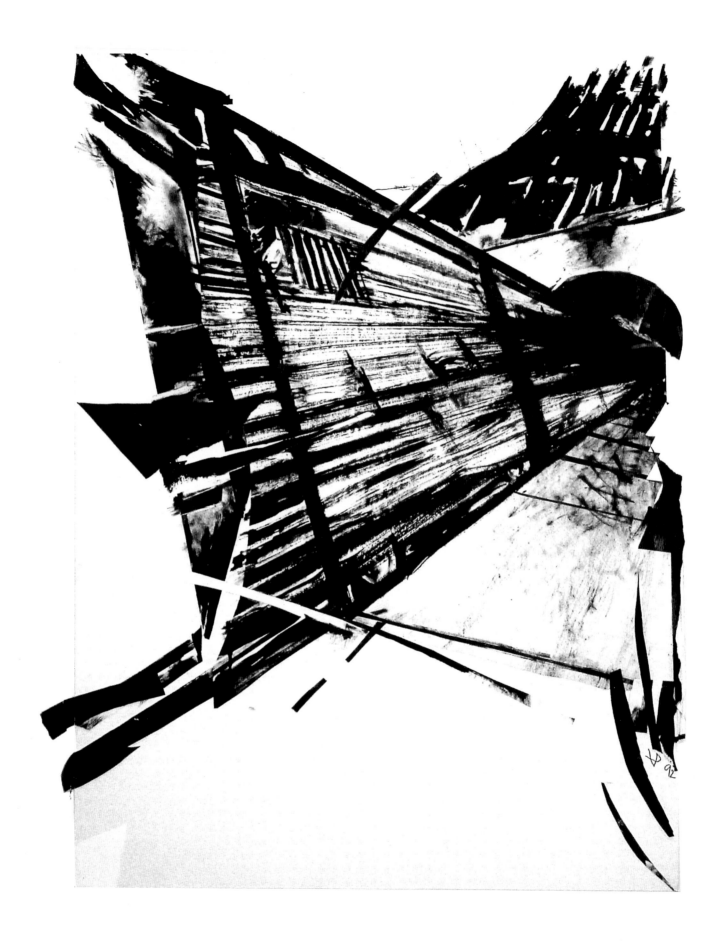

Smashed Window

Time and Window

Post Script.

Creating this exhibition has been a wonderful team effort. Bill Pachner has made himself and his studios wonderfully accessible. Geoff Simon (past Museum President) and Stephen Feinstein (FHM Consulting Curator of Art) have shepherded this exhibition from its initial concept two years ago to fruition – complete with video interviews, catalogue essays and a unique curatorial "eye." Ann Pachner, an artist and designer in her own right, has guided the Museum through the design and publishing of this handsome catalogue. The New York Poet Michael Perkins offers a personal tribute. The Museum curatorial team of Noreen Brand, Erin Blankenship, Karen Mibus and Kent Bontly have ensured that not only has the work been conserved, properly framed and mounted, but also photographed and installed with excellence and skill. But without the encouragement and unstinting and generous support of Jo and Bob Franzblau, none of this would have been possible. Thank you to all.

R. A. M.

PLATES

1. *Tracks*, tempera and collage on canvas, 47.75"x47.75", (1990) (cover).
5. William Pachner (photo: Jennifer Elliot).
8. *The Door*, tempera, 40"x30", (1984).
13. *Elegy for a City (Prague)*, watercolor on paper, 31"x28", (1975).
14. *His Spiritual Highness in a State of Moral Dilemma*, oil on masonite, 26"x30" (1949) (top).
14. *Inquisitor*, gouache on paper, 28"x19.5", (1946-1950), (bottom).
15. *German Train*, oil on board, 21"x28", (1944).
16. *A Word from Our Sponsor*, watercolor, pencil and ink on paper, 14"x11.75", (1962).
17. *A Group of Winning Sportsmen*, pen and ink on paper, 15.25"x11", (1953).
18. *Family by the Graveside*, gouache on board, 35.5"x23.5", (1955) (top).
18. *The Collector*, collage on board, 29"x20", (1961) (bottom).
19. *Double Portrait of the Artist*, ink and watercolor on paper, 17.5"x24", (1945) (top).
19. *Emigrant Portrait of the Artist*, pen and ink and collage on paper, 14"x10.25", (1961) (bottom).
21. *Tracks*, pen and ink and collage on board, 11"x14", (1966).
22. *Native Landscape*, oil on canvas, 35"x47", (1965).
23. *The Train*, oil on canvas, 48"x48", (1960).
24 *Spring Landscape*, oil on canvas, 36.5"x36.5" (1964).
31. *Door Opened and Slammed Shut*, tempera, 40"x30", (1993).
33. *Landscape of the River Sola*, oil on canvas, 72"x72", (1966).
35. *Summer Landscape*, oil on canvas, 70.5"x70.5", (1960-67).
37. *The Wood*, oil on canvas, 70.5"x70.5", (1980).
39. *Landscape*, oil on canvas, 60.25"x70.25", (1981).
40. *Italian Landscape*, collage and watercolor on paper, 30.25"x22", (1975).
41. *Imagined Landscape #2*, watercolor on paper, 20"x14" (1977).
43. *Terminal*, oil on canvas, 45"x44.75", (1975).
44 - 45. *Landscape of Crisis*, oil on canvas, 52"x77", (1964).
47. *Landscape, Entirely Man Made*, tempera, 47.75"x47.75", (1991).
48. *Howling Forest*, tempera, 44"x28", (1987).
49. *Scream*, tempera, 70"x68", (1989).
50. *Mercedes*, collage on canvas, 71.5"x61", (1988).
51. *Truck*, tempera, 82"x71", (1989).
52. *Locomotive-Freight Train*, tempera, 29"x23", (1992).
53. *Steam Engine*, collage on canvas, 48"x47.5", (1990).
54. *Train in Tunnel*, tempera, 40"x31", (1992).
55. *Night Freight*, collage on canvas, 62"x72", (1993).
56. *Smashed Window*, collage and tempera on paper, 60"x40", (1997).
57. *Time and Window*, tempera, 24"x36", (1990's).
58. *Of Memory and Forgetting*, collage and tempera on canvas, 70"x70", (1998).
72. *Gate and Door*, tempera, 38"x30", (1987-98).(back cover)

William Pachner *Chronology*

1915   Birth of Vilem (William) Pachner, son of Anna and Josef Pachner, in Brtnice, then Austro-Hungarian Empire, Czechoslovakia from 1919 until 1992, which on January 1, 1993, peacefully split into the Czech Republic and Slovakia.

1920   Rides in the cabin of a locomotive, a ride arranged by his grandfather, Leopold. Injures left eye while sharpening a pencil.

1920's   Doesn't excel in academic subjects, but some of his teachers allow him to pass because of his drawings. However, professional artists advise Anna Pachner that her son has no talent.

Enters the Kunstgewerbeschule, a design school in Vienna, and studies fashion illustration.

Wins first and second prizes for student fashion designs at Wiener Festwochen. Dissatisfied with academic routine, leaves design school and becomes an illustrator for Melantrich Publishing House in Prague.

1935   Becomes a staff artist for the Czechoslovak illustrated weekly, *Ozveny*.

1939   General Josef Bily, husband of Pachner's editor at *Ozveny*, arranges a temporary visa so that Pachner can visit America. Arrives in New York on March 9, learns of German occupation of Czechoslovakia. Travels to Chicago. Presents his work at *Esquire* magazine and is initially rejected, then hired.

1940   Becomes Art Director for *Esquire*, marries Lorraine Koolman (editor's secretary at *Esquire*), from Wellsburg, Iowa. (Children: Ann Koolman Pachner, b. 1944; and, Charles Edward Pachner, b. 1946).

1943   Leaves *Esquire* to enlist in the Army, but is rejected three times. Is determined to participate in the war effort, so makes anti-fascist illustrations for magazines such as *Collier's*, *Cosmopolitan*, and *Redbook*.

1944   Receives citation for Meritorious Service from the National War Fund. Has first solo exhibition at the Barry Stephens Gallery in New York.

1945   Receives confirmation that his entire family has been exterminated by the Nazis. Moves to Woodstock, New York and buys a house from Juliana Force, Director of the Whitney Museum of American Art.

1948   Has one-man show at the Weyhe Gallery. Begins to participate in large annual exhibitions, such as the Carnagie International and the Whitney Museum of American Art Annual.

1949   Receives citation and $1000 award from the National Institute of Arts and Letters for "masterful use of powerful design to express a deep emotional experience." Exhibits in the first two group shows at the Corcoran Gallery, Washington. Paintings are acquired by Milwaukee Art Institute; Witte Memorial Museum, San Antonio; Ein-harod Museum, Israel. Has one-man exhibition at A.A.A. Gallery in New York.

1950   Exhibits in first of two group shows at the Pennsylvania Academy of Fine Arts. Exhibits by invitation in Best of Art-New Directions in Town Hall, New York City for two consecutive years.

1951   Is invited to Florida to teach art by Mrs. Shillard Smith, founder of the Florida Gulf Coast Art Center. Establishes a winter residence on Clearwater Beach (until 1969). Has the first of two one-man exhibits at Ganso Gallery in New York.

1954   Has one-man exhibition at the Ringling Museum in Sarasota.

1957   Begins teaching at the Tampa Art Institute, and continues each winter until 1969. Establishes William Pachner Workshop, Clearwater. Participates in circulating exhibition, *Four Florida Painters*, sponsored by the American Federation of Arts.

1958   Receives $1000 Painting of the Year Award at the Atlanta Museum of Art. Receives First Prize, Art Association of New Orleans, 57th Spring Annual at the Issac Delgado Museum. Receives Purchase Prize, Sarasota Annual National Show. Receives First Prize, Florida State Fair Fine Arts Exhibition. Exhibits in *Art: USA: 58* in New York. Receives Guggenheim Fellowship, travels to Europe.

1959   Meets Martin Buber in Jerusalem. Has first retrospective exhibition, awarded by the American Federation of Arts and funded by a grant from the Ford Foundation. *Terminal Number 1* is purchased by the Whitney Museum of American Art. Has the first of several one-man exhibitions at the Krasner Gallery. Joseph H. Hirshhom purchases *Antinomes #1* and other works. Exhibits in group shows at the University of Nebraska, University of Michigan, and the Detroit Institute of Fine Arts. Receives one-man exhibition at the John and Mable Ringling Museum of Art, Sarasota.

1964   Receives grant from the Ford Foundation (one of a series of Museum residency grants for artists) and serves residency at the Fort Worth Art Museum.

1965   Exhibits in Fine Arts Pavilion at the New York World's Fair.

1966   Has one-man exhibition at Tampa Art Institute.

1967   Exhibits in group show at the New York Cultural Center.

1970-
80   Paints in Woodstock and makes only short annual trips to Tampa. Exhibits at Trend House Gallery, Tampa.

1974   Has one-man exhibition at the J. Camp Gallery in New York City.

1979-
80   Builds studio in Tampa.

1981   Loses sight in his "good" eye and becomes blind. Receives one-man show at the Scarfone Gallery, University of Tampa on January 8. Receives honorary Doctor of Fine Arts degree from University of Tampa. Resolves to continue working despite blindness. After experiments with color, does extensive series of drawings in B&W that focus on the memory of the Holocaust.

1983   Has one-man exhibition, *Pachner Landscapes,* at the Museum of Fine Arts, St. Petersburg, Florida.

1985   *Landscape & Lovers,* watercolors and drawings from 50s to 70s; first solo exhibition at Brad Cooper Gallery.

1987   Has retrospective exhibition, *William Pachner Affirmations: 1936-1986,* Tampa, Museum of Art. Solo exhibition, *William Pachner: Affirmations Black and White,* University of South Florida Galleries, Tampa. *Drawings: Quiet Revolution*, group exhibition at Brad Cooper Galley with James Rosenquist, Theo Wujcik, and Irwin Touster.

1988   Solo exhibition at the Arts Center in St. Petersburg: a survey of B&W works in January. Solo exhibition at Brad Cooper Gallery in December of *Small Works: Watercolors from the Years 1964-82*. (1982 was the year working in color came to an end for Pachner) Group exhibition at the Brad Cooper Gallery exhibiting B&W work *Variations on an Unstated Theme*.

1990   Solo exhibition at Brad Cooper Gallery: *Recent Works, 1980-1990: The First Decade*, of Pachner working with black ink on white paper and canvas in March.

1991   Inaugural Group Exhibition at new location of Brad Cooper Gallery, exhibits *Truck*, 1989 (large B&W painting) Painter James Rosenquist purchases *Truck*.

1992   *Collage Constructions*, solo exhibition of new black and white works encompassing the continuously evolving variations on Pachner's themes at Brad Cooper Gallery in April. Summer group exhibition at Brad Cooper Gallery.

1993   *The Florida Landscape Revisited*, five 19th Century and sixteen contemporary artists investigate the Florida environment as a cultural landscape: Polk Museum of Art, Lakeland, Florida. *Group One*, exhibition at Brad Cooper Gallery.

1994   *Selected Early Works, 1956-1978*, a solo exhibition at Brad Cooper Gallery of pastels, watercolors, oils, and drawings. *Drawings, Discovery & Diversity*, group exhibition at Brad Cooper Gallery.
        Oils and Watercolors 1960-1980, solo exhibition at Brad Cooper Gallery

1995   His wife Lorraine dies of leukemia at her home in Woodstock. Bill and Lorraine were married for fifty five years.

1996   Mackey Gallery at the Museum of Fine Art in St. Petersburg exhibits work from permanent collection.

2000   *William Pachner: Painting & Drawing; A Selection of Works from the 1960's*; paintings, pastels, and drawings, solo exhibition at the Brad Cooper Gallery in January. *16th Anniversary Group*, at Brad Cooper Gallery.

2003   *Modern Art in Florida, 1948-1970*, Tampa Museum of Art, Tampa, Florida.

2004   Solo exhibition at Brad Cooper Gallery, *Selected Works 1960-1970*

Pachner *Bibliography*

Bennett, Lennie. "Season in the Sun". St. Petersburg, FL. *St. Petersburg Times,* May 16, 2004.

Brad Cooper Galleries web page: *Gallery I William Pachner*
April 24 – June 26, 2004. http://www.bradcoopergallery.com/wpachner_6.html

Donahue, Kenneth. *William Pachner.* New York. The American Federation of Arts, 1959.

Fort Worth Museum of Art. *Work of William Pachner,* May 11 - May 31, 1964

Martin, Robert. *Pachner Landscapes.* Museum of Fine Arts, St. Petersburg, FL. February 13 through March 27, 1983.

Nichols, Bradley J. *William Pachner: Affirmations 1936-1986.* Tampa, FL. Tampa Museum of Art. February 22-
April 19, 1987.

Stern, Guy and Brigitte Suman. *William Pachner, A Painter from Prague, Vienna and Florida,* in *Exile Literature
and Other Arts: International Conference on German and Austrian Exiles, 1933-1945.* Department of Germanic and
Slavic Languages and Literatures, University of Florida, March 10-13, 1988.

Statement by William Pachner

"The Basis of Art" a chapter in *Art of the Artist,* Arthur Zaidenberg, ed. New York. Crown, 1951. pp. 136-139.

Exhibition Catalogues

New York City. Barry Stephens Gallery. *William Pachner: exhibition of paintings and illustrations,* Ap 6-27, 1945.
4p. Gallery imprint.

New York City. Associated American Artists. *Three Paintings by William Pachner,* Ja 10-29, 1949. 4p. 1 il.
Gallery imprint.

Sarasota. The John and Mable Ringling Museum of Art. *Four Painters: Eugene Massin, William Pachner,
Syd Solomon, Karl Zerbe,* Ap 2-My 31, 1957. 19 p. 3 Pachner il. Museum imprint.

PERIODICALS

Coast to Coast Reports on Current Exhibitions. Art Digest, 26:13 D 1, 1951.

Fifty-Seventh Street in Review. Art Digest, 25:18 Ja 15, 1951.

Fortnight in Review. Arts Digest 29:23 Ja 1, 1955. 1 il.

Gibbs, Jo. *Lest We Forget.* Art Digest 22:13 Ja 15, 1948. 1 il.

Season's Previes. Art Digest 20:18 Ag 1946. 1 il.

In the Galleries. Arts 33:62 F 1959.

Mass Magazines Promoting Fine Art. Arts Digest 25:13 Ja 1, 1951. 1 il.

Redbook Commissions Fine Art. American Artist 15:71 F 1951. 1 il.

Reviews and Previews. Art News 46:43 Ja 1948, *Arts News* 49:50 O 1950, *Arts News* 49:47 Ja 1951, *Arts News* 53:65 F 1955, *Arts News* 57:52 F 1959.

Rosh Hashana and Yom Kippur. (Illustration commissioned for series on religious holidays, colored reproduction made available for framing.) *Redbook* 95:34 S 1950.

Sharpe, Marynell. *American Academy and National Institute Honor Artists.* Art Digest 23:11 Je 1949. 1 il.

Soby, James Thrall. *Contemporary Painting at the Whitney Museum of American Art. Saturday Review of Literature* 33:74 D2, 1950.

Song of the United Nations (illustration). *Esquire* 18:32,59 D 1942.

"Three Paintings and a Group of Drawings at Associated American Artists Gallery". *Art News* 47:48 Ja 1949.

AND enumerable articles in Tampa, St Petersburg and other Florida News Papers.

1

2

3

4

5

6

7

8

9

1. *The Road*,ᵃ 32″x40″, 1983.
2. *Interrogation Room*,ᵃ 24″x19″, 1983.
3. *End of the Line*,ᵃ 32″x40″, 1983.

4. *Scream*,ᵃ 40″x30.25″, 1985.
5. *Self-Portrait*,ᵇ 24″x19″, 1985.
6. *Suitcase*,ᵃ 36″x43″, 1988-98.

7. *The Door Metaphor*,ᵃ 40″x30″, 1992.
8. *Table*,ᵃ 82″x72″, 1988.
9. *Truck 2*,ᵃ 68″x68″, 1989.

a. tempera.   b. acrylic on paper

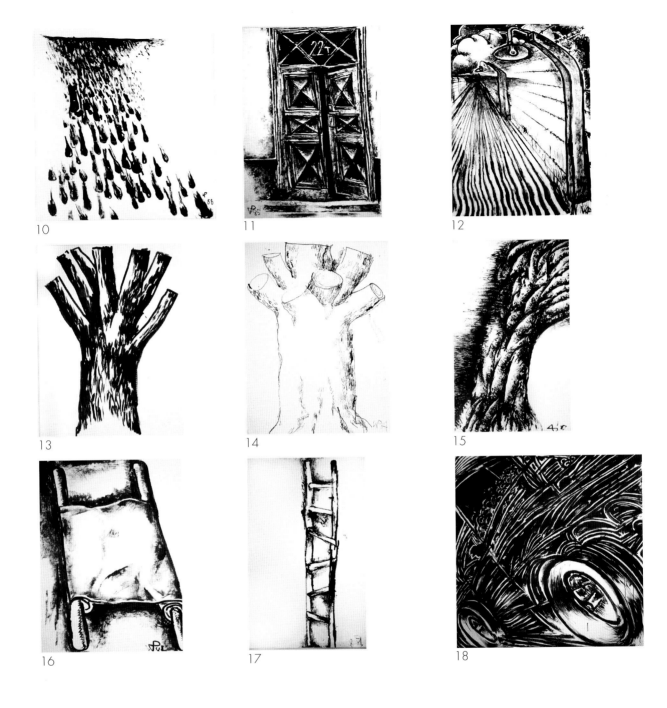

68

10. *Composition*,ᵃ 29"x23", 1988.
11. *Door II*,ᵃ 40"x30.5", 1983.
12. *Camp Lights*,ᵃ 40"x30.5", 1984.

13. *Tree*,ᵃ 24"x19", 1984.
14. *Tree*,ᵃ 24"x19", 1984.
15. *Tree in a Storm*,ᵃ 44"x28", 1987.

16. *'Scroll*,ᵃ 40"x30.5", 1984.
17. *Ascent of Man*,ᵃ 38"x25", 1989.
18. *Truck*,ᵃ 70"x70", 1987.

a. tempera.

19

20

21

22

23

24

25

26

27

19. *An Eagle of a Man,* c 40"x30.5".
20. *A Relationshio Based on Mutual Esteem,* c 10"x8".
21. *There Are Two Sides to Every Story,* c

14.75"x11.25", 1952.
22. *Entrance,* 8"x10".
23. *Everyone Repeat After Me,* c 15"x11.25".
24 *Homage,* c 8"x10".

25. *Life's Dream Achieved,* c 15.25"x11".
26. *Our Lord Knows Who Are the Godly 1953,* c 15.25"x11".
27. *Ethics Be Damed,* c 15"x11".

c. pen and ink on paper.